My Story
Of
Domestic Violence

My Story Of Domestic Violence

Linda Jensen

LIBERTY HILL PUBLISHING

Liberty Hill Publishing
555 Winderley Pl, Suite 225
Maitland, FL 32751
407.339.4217
www.libertyhillpublishing.com

Paperback ISBN-13: 979-8-86850-544-7
Ebook ISBN-13: 979-8-86850-545-4

This story begins with a young lady named Faith from New York. At twenty years old, Faith was pursuing her degree in cosmetology, styling hair. When that didn't work out, she moved on. Faith lived with her parents, Ben and Sandra. She took some time off to run around and find out who she was and what the big world had to offer. Faith met many friends throughout her journey. She met a very special man, Chad, and they became close. Faith wasn't very experienced in what men desired, but she learned very quickly what Chad wanted. He was experienced and much older than Faith. One night, Chad moved close to Faith and started kissing her. She moved away quickly. Chad pulled her back and started undressing her, letting her clothes drop to the floor and gently laying her on the bed. He got on top of her. Faith whispered "Stop, I am not ready for this!" Chad held her down against her will, got on top of Faith and began pleasuring her. Faith had never done this sort of thing before. She was scared of what was going to happen, but Chad continued. He then whispered to Faith, "I can't believe I have found such a highly intelligent, witty, and beautiful woman that I am very attracted to." When they had finished what they were doing, Faith noticed there was blood on the sheets. Chad said "Well, you're not a virgin anymore, my dear." As time went on, Faith wasn't feeling well. She was having morning sickness, so she went to the doctor's office to see what was wrong. She was scared of what she might find. The doctor examined her, only to find out she was pregnant. Faith was frightened at the thought of it. She didn't know what she was going to do. She thought she better get a hold of Chad and tell him she was pregnant, so Faith called Chad to let him know. His response was, " I don't need another child, my child is grown." Faith replied, "I don't need your help!" She went home to tell her parents she was pregnant. Thank goodness for Faith's loving parents who said she could stay with them and have her child. This was all new to Faith. She was scared, but she knew she had to start buying baby items. On the night of April 12, 1984, Faith started having contractions as she laid on her parents couch. Her little sister, Bella, kept track of her contractions. When it got close, Faith's father took her to the hospital and dropped Faith off at the front door where she met her friend Jackie, so she wouldn't have to go through it alone. On April 13, 1984, a baby boy was born to Faith. She named him Caleb. The nurse put him in her arms. Faith said he was so adorable and tiny. Her father picked Faith up at the hospital to bring her back to their house. Her mother, Sandra, helped her so much with Caleb; she loved him as one of her own. Caleb would stay with Sandra when Faith would go out for the night. It happened quite often. Faith met Jackson at the bar. He was flirting with Faith, they danced, and had a wonderful evening. Faith was falling for Jackson. Her life changed when she fell in love with him. She began to date him and everything was going great. Jackson worked for Dayton's Trucking Company. Faith would talk to Jackson every day. Jackson would always go to the bar after work. Faith began to worry if Jackson would meet someone else. He would never admit it; he would always say he just had a couple beers with the guys. Faith had her suspicions that something was going on. Faith then decided to go about her life. She wasn't going to waste it on Jackson. She started spending more time with her son. He was growing so fast and Faith knew she was missing out on too much. But just as Faith was getting along, Jackson would call and want to do something and Faith would drop everything she was doing and take off to be by his side. Jackson had been wanting to ask Faith if she would marry him, but he wanted to do it on his own terms. He didn't want to ask her in person. He wanted to call her and ask her on the phone and that is what he did. Faith said "Yes, yes I will marry you. I have never been married before." Faith was so happy she didn't even give it any thought that she said "yes". Jackson said, "I have some conditions. We will get married in the court house. There will be no big wedding." Faith didn't care; she loved Jackson so much that she was okay with not having a big wedding. Sandra, Faith's mother, tried to talk her out of it because she had heard from different sources that he wasn't a good man. But Faith would not listen to anyone; she wanted to be married to Jackson. So on June 19, 1986, Faith and Jackson got married. Afterwards, they met friends and family at the local bar and they celebrated their happy day. After a while, Jackson decided they were going to leave and head home. Jackson lived in Cedar Woods so it was a little drive to get there. Faith was nervous and anxious at the same time. She wasn't very experienced in the lovemaking department. Jackson was a blunt man; he would say what was on his mind and you better do it. When they arrived home, they went in the house that Jackson was living in with a friend. His friend had the upstairs and Jackson had the downstairs. Right away, Jackson wanted to have sex. He said, "Woman, get in the bedroom and get your clothes off and get in bed."

He got on top of Faith and had his way with her. Jackson let it be known that he was experienced in the bedroom and he knew that she wasn't. He would say "talk to your friends or look it up in the library." It was humiliating to her. Faith knew as life went on that things wouldn't change much with Jackson. He liked to be in control of everything. He would still go out with his friends to the bar at night leaving Faith and Caleb home alone and not come home until he felt like it. Her feelings began to change towards Jackson. He would come home from the bar and want to fight and if she dared ask how his night went, he would say it was none of her business. The next day after work, Jackson came home and informed her that they were moving. Jackson said,

"So you need to start getting this house packed up." Faith was happy. It would be their first house together and Caleb would be joining them. Faith thought Jackson would come home more often. Jackson and Caleb were getting along very well. He treated Caleb as if he was his own. Faith thought Jackson would come home the first night in the new house, but Faith spent another night alone. Faith was getting to the point where she wanted so badly to ask Jackson where the hell he was, but she knew better because it would start a fight. Faith began to think there was more going on that was not being talked about.

She decided she would go to the bar the next night to check it out and see what was so important. Jackson didn't want Faith's friends coming around the house. It was okay for family to visit, but not friends. She had to give up every-thing and couldn't visit her parents unless she asked. After telling her to pack the house, Jackson brought up the fact that she needed to find a job and help out. He said he couldn't do it on his own any-more, but he would pay rent and the rest of his money would go in his account. I called my friend, Marie, to see if she would check around to see if there were any job openings at her place of employ-ment. Faith had to find daycare. She was so scared because she hadn't had to work before. Jackson said he had someone for daycare. He had known her for many years and Caleb would be safe. Faith agreed to it. Jackson bluntly said that she would be paying for the daycare and the bills that came in. Faith was getting tired of waiting to hear something from the Golden Packing Plant so she called the plant and she found out she had gotten the job. Faith made plans to ride to work with Marie, which pissed Jackson off. He didn't like Marie and didn't want her around. Faith told him that was her ride to work and to lay off. Faith was so excited to tell Jackson she had gotten the job, but Jackson didn't come home as usual. Faith had enough. She put on her coat, took Caleb to her mother's house, and went to the bar where Jackson hung out. Faith was very nervous and scared to see what was going on, so she went into the bar and looked around. She found Jackson close to another woman dancing. Faith didn't know if she should go or stay and face Jackson. Faith decided to leave the bar. She was scared that Jackson would embarrass her in front everyone, but now she knew what Jackson was up to -no good. Faith went back home, took a shower and went to bed. There was no reason to stay up and share any good news with him. Jackson came home and woke Faith up. He said, "What the hell are you checking up on me for!!" Faith sat up in bed and just knew there was a fight to begin. "I wanted to find out what was so important. You have to go to the bar every night and I saw with my own eyes you hugging another woman dancing with her, so you can go to hell!" Faith responded. Jackson got into bed and tried to pull Faith close to him. She told him to leave her alone. Jackson begged her saying he was sorry and that Faith was the only woman he needed. Faith overlooked it like nothing happened. She loved Jackson so much. Jackson told Faith to get undressed and get back in bed. Jackson would get on top of her and pleasure her and then himself. The next morning, Faith told Jackson that she got the job and would be starting that day. Jackson asked where Caleb was, and she told him that she had taken him to her mother's house. Jackson said that Caleb didn't need to be going down there all the time and that he was just spoiled. Faith said that she would take him there any time she pleased, and she left for work. Faith got to work and she didn't feel very well, but stayed and did her job. Her stomach hurt and there was a burning sensation from her throat to her stomach. Faith was getting scared and she couldn't figure out what was wrong. Marie took Faith home and then left. Faith went in and laid down on the couch and fell asleep. Jackson came home to find no supper on the table and Faith sleeping on the couch. Jackson woke her up and said, "Get me some supper going!" Faith said, "I can't, I don't feel well at all." Jackson said, "Go to bed, it will go away and I'll fix my own dinner." Well during the night the pain had gotten worse. Faith wanted to go to the hospital but Jackson said, "I am not taking you to the hospital, roll over and go to sleep." Faith couldn't, so she got up and called her friend Marie to see if she would take her to the hospital.

She came right over. Well, it was a good thing Faith went to the hospital. It was her gallbladder the whole time. Faith was in the hospital and Jackson did not visit. He was going with the guys to the bar.

When Faith did get home, she took it easy until she felt better. Jackson came home and told Faith that he ran into a guy who had a bigger house to rent, so they needed to start packing and move at the end of the month. Faith couldn't help because she still didn't feel well. Jackson lacked empathy and Faith was seeing how controlling he was becoming. As soon as Faith started feeling better, she started packing. After Faith and Jackson moved and got their new house put together, there was more room. Faith quit her job at Golden Packing Plant and took an evening job so Jackson could be with Caleb at night and she could be with him during the day. This would work out perfectly. That is, until Jackson decided not come home at night. Jackson continued to go out to the bar. Jackson's attitude was changing and he was becoming more hostile. Jackson wasn't home when Faith had to be to work so she had no other choice but to go over to the neighbor's house across the driveway to ask if they could babysit Caleb until Jackson could get home. They were delighted to, so Faith went on to work not knowing trouble was headed her way. It was Faith's lunch time along with her co-worker's. The lunch room had all glass windows in it. As she and her co-worker's were eating, they all heard a hard knock on the window. It was Jackson. Faith was surprised and unsettled, going outside to talk to Jackson. Faith asked Jackson ''What the hell are you doing?" Faith was embarrassed in front of her co-workers. Jackson replied, "Where did you take Caleb?" She responded, "To the neighbor's house cause you couldn't bring yourself home from the bar." Jackson replied, "Which one of those guys did you have sex with?" Faith said, "I need you to leave and don't come back!!" As Jackson was leaving, he threw a beer can at the window of the lunch room. Faith hadn't seen this sort of behavior before and was scared to return home. When she entered the house, she found Jackson lying on the couch like nothing happened. Faith just walked by him, not speaking to him the rest of the day. She took Caleb and laid him down in his bed and she laid down in her bed. Jackson came into the bedroom where Faith was and said how sorry he was. Faith said, "I am tired of your sorry ass." Faith knew he wasn't sorry because he would continue to accuse her of looking and being with other men. Jackson started an argument with Caleb when he was only eight years old, so being scared of Jackson, he ran out the door bare-footed down the street to his grand-mother's house. Faith ran out the door after Caleb. She got in her car and went to her parents' house to find Caleb there crying. Faith decided to stay at her moth-er's house in the middle of the night. At some point, Jackson came down and took a part off the car so Faith wouldn't be able to go anywhere. She told her mother that she married the wrong man. He was becoming a different person. During the whole mess, Faith found out she was pregnant and was going to have another child. Faith called Jackson the next day and told him she was moving out. That made Jackson furious. He wanted his family all back in the same house. Faith's father Ben fixed Faith's car the very next day and then pulled it up inside the driveway, locked it up and closed the gate. Jackson came down to Faith's parents' house pounding on Faith's window. She told him to go away or they would call the police. Jackson was begging Faith to come home. He was very sorry and it would never happen again. Jackson was good at saying sorry to get his way. Faith was always forgiving and taking Jackson back. Faith left Caleb at her parents' house. The next day, Faith went down to Jackson's place of employment to tell him she was pregnant in person. Faith approached Jackson and told him she was pregnant. Jackson didn't have much to say. But of course he didn't come home again, so Faith just went to bed because she had work the next day. By the time Faith was ready to have the baby and go to the hospital, Jackson took her stay just till the baby was born It was a boy! They named him Foster. Faith never saw Jackson again until she returned home. Her father Ben picked her up. Faith was fed up with Jackson. Foster and Caleb were growing up into young boys. Faith would have loved to stay home and take care of them, but she knew that couldn't happen. The very next day, when Jackson came home from work, he told Faith they were moving and the house needed to be packed by the end of the month. Faith said, "I just had a baby, I need some time to heal." Jackson's behavior was changing even more. He wasn't the man she married. Faith couldn't figure out what was going on with him, so she just asked him what his problem was. He said he didn't have good news. The shop was going under and that they weren't getting their paychecks. Jackson and Faith sat down and talked about what they were going to do. Jackson was always was good with painting and working on cars, so he thought he could work out of the garage and Foster and Caleb could stay home with Jackson. This would save on daycare. Faith was thinking of a way she could stay home and take care of her children. Jackson sat down to listen to Faith and she said, she could do daycare and be home with her children. Jackson agreed to it so Faith advertised in the paper. She also had friends that needed daycare for their children. Faith wasn't aware of all the people in and out of the garage all night long. Faith was wondering what was going on. The babysitting business was going very well. Faith would take the children to school every morning on time, Jackson would come in the house often to see the children, and sometimes Jackson would stay with the smaller children, so Faith didn't have to take them along to pick the older children at school. Faith was surprised he did that for her. Jackson started changing in a scary kind of way. He started going back to the bars and taking his boat out, inviting a lot of other woman to go along. Faith always had the children and wouldn't allow them on the river, so she would stay home, not knowing what was going on. They were always late coming back, then they would go back to the bar. One night, Faith walked over to the bar. It was only across the street and she saw Jackson's van. She looked inside the van only to find Jackson passed out sitting in the back of the van with his pants down to his ankles. Faith was furious!! She got into the driver's seat, threw the van in reverse and spun out of the parking lot throwing Jackson around in the back of the van. Faith hit the sewer, went up over and landed back down into the street. She went around the corner doing 30 miles per hour and threw Jackson on the floor of the van. When Faith got home, she threw the van in to park and left Jackson in the van to sober up and realize what he had done. Faith went in the house, locking the doors behind her, then she got dressed for bed and went to bed. As Faith lay in bed, she thought how her suspicions were right about Jackson. He was cheating on her and she found out much more that night. There was crystal meth on the table in the van. Faith had heard that meth was a highly addictive drug. Faith was ready to call it quits. It was strange how things were happening, especially around the house. Faith noticed cameras on the garage which weren't there when they moved in. There were cameras on the house that weren't there before. Jackson placed small tape recorders in the two vans she drove, so he could hear what was going on in the van when she drove it. You could hear the little children making noises. She didn't know he was following her to the schools to drop off the children, because he thought she was meeting other men. He must have been feeling his own guilt of what he did. Jackson would also put a recorder in his van in the street, pointing it towards the house and putting two big spot lights on the house. Jackson followed Faith on shopping trips with her friends and mother. He would embarrass her in front of her mom and friends by yelling at her whether she was with other men. Faith was starting to lose the love she had for Jackson. That night, Jackson came home in a rage and told her to sit down on the couch and listen to this tape out of the van she drove. Jackson said, "listen closely; it sounds like you're having sex in the van." Faith got up said, "you are losing your mind!" Jackson pushed her back down on couch and said, "you're not going anywhere until you listen to this tape and tell me what's going on." Faith told him it was the children in the van. It didn't do her any good to defend herself, Jackson wasn't listening. Faith was yelling at him to listen, but he was convinced she was cheating. Jackson would deny he was on drugs. He would stay home with the younger children so Faith could take the older children to school. Faith laid out blankets so they could rest and watch a movie. Jackson came across a feather that was on one of the blankets. He swore it was a feather off one of my lingerie sets. Faith said, "how the hell am I going to have sex in my lingerie with children here?" She began to think, "who is this monster I married!" It was getting a little scary. Faith wasn't feeling very well, she was very stressed and sick to her stomach. She had felt this feeling before when she was pregnant. She made a doctor's appointment. The doctor said she was under a lot of stress and needed to settle down. Faith began to tell her doctor what was going on. She advised Faith to get out, but after the pap smear saying she was pregnant, she had no way of leaving Jackson. Yet, the doctor asked if Jackson had been cheating on her. Faith said "yes", and the doctor said that explained the infections she had been getting. The doctor told her to stop having sex with Jackson, but that was easier said than done. The doctor said Jackson needed to get some help soon. It was such a bad time to end up pregnant. Faith got home and went in the garage to tell Jackson she was pregnant again and Jackson spoiled it all. He asked Faith if she had been in his garage having sex because there were fingerprints in the sanding dust on the car he was working on. Jackson said they were not his and she had better explain since she was the only one with a key to the garage. Faith was angry. She told him they were not her fingerprints and he could have his damn key. Faith said, "I came in here to tell you that you were going to be a father again." Faith went in the house and sat on the couch and just cried and cried, not knowing what to do. As Faith was sitting on the couch looking out the sliding glass window, she saw Foster push Caleb and run to his dad, telling him Caleb pushed him. Jackson came up on the deck and grabbed Caleb by the neck. Faith went running out and told Jackson, "Stop!! And don't ever touch him again." She took Caleb down to her mother's house until she could figure out what needed to be done. Faith went to the garage and pounded on the door until Jackson opened it. She told him that if he ever touched one of her children again, she would call the police. Jackson said that she would not want to do that. Jackson had put locks on the outside of the doors so Faith couldn't get out at night. In Jackson's mind, he thought she was getting out at night running around with men. Faith was finding burnt foil in the bathroom, bedroom, and the bathroom in the bedroom. She knew it had to do with something with the drug Jackson was taking. That night, she had gone out on the porch to pick up all the toys and straighten up and just happened to look to the side. Jackson was in the driveway, down on his hands and knees taking pictures of the tire tracks in the driveway. She knocked on the window since she couldn't get out the door. Jackson looked up and asked who was over while he was gone. Faith told him he was out of his mind and crazy. After nine months passed, Faith was in labor and Jackson was nowhere to be found. Her water had broken, and she drove herself to the hospital. They had to stop the labor because the baby's lungs weren't developed. They transferred her to another hospital in New York. She was alone. She was having contractions, ready to have the baby, and Jackson was still not there. Faith had a gut feeling he was with someone. On her last push, Jackson came waltzing in like nothing was wrong. She was so angry, she didn't talk to Jackson. Faith rested and had something to eat. Since Damien's lungs weren't developed, the doctor said he would have to stay four weeks in a NICU at the hospital. Faith stayed in the hospital for three nights. Since Damien had to stay in the hospital, she was there every day. Jackson would drop her off without coming to see his child. The day Damien got of the hospital, Jackson picked them up and dropped them off at home.

After Jackson got home, Faith told him to sit down and that they needed to talk. She asked Jackson, "Are you cheating on me? I want to know now!" Jackson became irate. Faith said she would find out. All she need to do was ask around. She told him she wanted a divorce. He went downstairs to where their bedroom was and took a knife and cut the waterbed all the way across. Water was going everywhere. Then he took a permanent black marker and in big letters he wrote IF I CAN'T HAVE YOU KNOW ONE WILL HAVE YOU!! Faith had to get to a phone since she couldn't use hers. Jackson had wired it to the garage, so she ran upstairs. Jackson grabbed her leg. She was kicking Jackson; he still had the knife in his hand. She got away, ran out the door and started yelling for help. The neighbor heard her yelling and said to come over and use her phone to call the police. Finally, Faith called the police. There were four cop cars that showed up. She told the police what Jackson had done and showed them the bedroom. The police took pictures of everything and took Jackson to jail. The next day, Faith went and got a protection order so Jackson could not come around the house at all. Jackson came right to the house when he got out of jail. She had told him he could not be there. It was so hot and he was sweating. She told him to leave again, but ended up having to call the police. They came and told him to get what he wanted now and he was to stay away from the house. But Jackson came back. He locked the children and Faith in the house from the outside, then he went over to the side of the house and cut the tubing to the air conditioner so it wouldn't work. Then he took the front gate off and took the hose. In the meantime he was yelling, "Take that you bitch, now who is going to sweat!" She couldn't get out of the house to call the police. She was locked in and was stuck until someone would show up. The mothers for whom Faith babysat started showing up around six o'clock. Finally one of the mothers opened the door. Faith used her phone to call the police to come to the house. Faith began to talk to the mothers and told them they shouldn't leave their children in the house. It was too dangerous. So, the mothers started pulling their children out of Faith's daycare for their own safety. The police showed up and Faith showed them what Jackson had done. The police took the information and gave her a blue card and told her she would probably be going to court over this. The police said they would try to find him and lock him up in jail. In the meantime, Faith talked to her brother, Mitch. He told her that he knew who Jackson was messing around with. It was Mitch's ex-girlfriend, Desiree. Faith was so angry that she called Desiree to find out what was going on. Desiree answered the phone and Faith asked if she was having sex with Jackson. Her response was, he slept on the couch and she slept in her bed, but locked the door so Jackson couldn't get in. Faith told her that if she thought she was stupid, she could have the lying bastard. Faith's mother had talked about getting a lawyer and told her to get the hell out of there before she was killed. Faith made an appointment to see a real good lawyer with a good reputation. She had the tapes that Jackson used to put in her van and the pictures from the bedroom. Faith went to court and her lawyer was great. She gave it to him. He had to do some jail time and whatever he took he would have to give back. He was now court-ordered to stay away from Faith, her house, and children. She had the locks removed from the outside of the doors, and tried hard to remain in the house. But, Jackson wouldn't leave her alone. So eventually, Faith took her children and moved. She didn't tell anyone, and to this day Jackson has not found their new location. They have been safe so far.

I share my story to highlight the reality of domestic violence. If one girl could be safe because they read this and understand the red flags, I will be happy. Don't wait to the last minute. Get help now. Find resources and talk to the police. Nothing will change unless you change it.